Nicki Jackowska has lived in Cornwall and Brighton. An early training in theatre, work as an actress, two university degrees and continuous inter-action with visual artists, musicians and performers have all influenced the writing in her ten published books. The most recent, *Write for Life* (Element 1997), is a radical exploration of language, identity and relationship.

Writing is her main occupation and has gained her numerous awards for both fiction and poetry.

She is currently researching a fourth novel, creating a new collection, tutoring and, as a student of analytical psychology, preparing a book on Jung and lost worlds.

She has one daughter, Laura, who also lives in Brighton.

Also by Nicki Jackowska

POETRY
The House that Manda Built
(The Menard Press 1981)

Earthwalks
(Ceolfrith Press 1982)

Letters to Superman
(Rivelin Grapheme 1984)

Gates to the City
(Taxus Press 1985)

News from the Brighton Front
(Sinclair-Stevenson 1993)

FICTION
Doctor Marbles and Marianne – A Romance
(Harvester 1982)

The Road to Orc
(Bran's Head Books 1985)

The Islanders
(Harvester 1987)

NON-FICTION
Write for Life
(Element Books 1997)

NICKI JACKOWSKA

Lighting a Slow Fuse

NEW AND SELECTED POEMS

London
ENITHARMON PRESS
1998

First published in 1998
by the Enitharmon Press
36 St George's Avenue
London N7 0HD

Distributed in Europe
by Littlehampton Book Services
through Signature Book Representation
2 Little Peter Street
Manchester M15 4PS

Distributed in the USA and Canada
by Dufour Editions Inc.
PO Box 7, Chester Springs
PA 19425, USA

ISBN 1 900564 11 4

British Library Cataloguing-in-Publication Data.
A catalogue record for this book is available
from the British Library.

ACKNOWLEDGEMENTS

Some of the new poems in *Under Cover*, the final
section of the book, have appeared in the following:
Gown Magazine (Belfast), *Klaonica: Poems for Bosnia* (Bloodaxe Books, 1993),
The Observer, *Poetry Review*, *Stand*, and the anthology
The Entertainers

Set in 10.5 on 13 Bembo by Bryan Williamson, Frome,
and printed in Great Britain by
The Cromwell Press, Wiltshire

For Marcus

'Love calls us back from simplification'
EAVAN BOLAND

CONTENTS

From *Gates to the City* (Taxus Press 1985)

From *News from the Brighton Front* (Sinclair-Stevenson 1993)

Under Cover: New Poems

MY MASTER COMES AND GOES

1

The master is here. He quite overcomes me.
He cries like a baby in the first shallows
And must be stroked awake
Out of his mad head. His bed is nettles
That kiss and silk his nightwalks
Through passages that run with stings.
He is a giant beetle with luminous green back
I can ride to sweetmeats and ripe gardens.

2

Later he grows. He changes colour even.
His coat is pitted with ends of rainbows,
They drive spears from their colour-tournaments
Through his space, and colours run
On his wet landscapes washed ambers and cerise.
Sometimes he curls and draws in his parts
And comes back hard and perfect like a marble bullet
Straight to the heart. The caught milkwhorl
Explodes, and it rains through the cavities
With milk like blossom.
In this hard round ball, he crashes through
Flesh like a painted bull.

3

He is a flower in an eggshell that waits its time.
The faces are hatched over mine,
They wobble and tease
And I can no longer be sure of the mirror.
When there is no other sound
He presses against my eardrums and whispers his charm,
His feet dance down my ears
Their patter is the distant click of a cricket.

4

He leaves in the last flutter of a drowned moth,
In the coiled spring of life, spiralling out.

5

My master uncurls ribbons out of your mouth,
He unravels slowly.
Your tongue is a pink lizard
Which is his finger.
The noise it points is the music of stones
And the notes settle and form,
They are gleaming monuments in wordbeds of stones.

6

He is the barbed elf, the branded head,
The single eye in a ruby chalice,
The peachcore, the thorn that laughs as it bites.
The locked box of dreams, with twin mice to guard it,
The split moon, the green edge of a flameface.
He is the hippopotamus with a snake's head,
The frog with a violin in its mouth,
The right piece of the cake,
The ripped buglenote of petrified town band.
He is the tree that yawns its trunk and bellows leaves,
The rose that will not bloom quiet.
He is a fruit of fur,
He is the happy creak of the splintered cross,
The right-handed lily,
The budding limb that the head grows
To find new places.
He is tumbled head and crumbling stone,
The witches joke, the trick of wizards,
The mirror, the splinter, the shriek, the cat,
He is the broken pattern in an old carpet of dust.

SOLSTICE

Candles bursting
out of my head
The loose wolf of sorrow
snuffling under my skirts

Bending under illegal air
A banishment

Moving among grasses
wearing badges of failure
I come to the crepuscule
mad country of the moth

SHE TRIES

She tries it many times
flaps at her wings and oils the carpet with sweat.
It pours rivers through the boards
and still she is floorbound.

She is a crow. A plain bird.
Ninetynine blinks of a black wing
won't fly her. On the floor
are rusty chalkmarks; she needs
to get very close to read what
they say, they are so familiar.

They keep her caged upstairs;
the lining is torn on the living-room
curtains, where she tried to get out.
She has raven's hair, and they say
she's too old to wear it loose like that.

Sometimes a song will ooze through
the pores of the house, and her
croak is of joy. Then she has
carved an arc to the ceiling, there
are a few feathers where the plaster cracks.

ANCIENT VOICES OF THE CHILDREN

The mouth is crying
like a sack of bones
In the rivers of autumn
the mouth weeps for it

Leaves scuttle and worry
on the edge of history
like crabs or a sea-shock
Through them, the rib

Children a naked memory
for the floral skirts
For ice in august
this pristine hymn

Ancient voices of the
children, rubbing their
soft curse against the ear
catching the new-made tear

STONES ON MONDAY

We are seven
stonegates waiting through time
recording the heartbeat of the shore

1
Maps of my ancestral home
I face you, faceless
the palest of skin and rusty hieroglyphs

2
I am kissed by a tree
a thumb print
the blue lace rides my birdback
I carry the word with me from the sea

3
Red is of iron, of claws
red, for interior, brown sea-blood
I was wet when you picked me, red as a flare
now I put forth small glittering surfaces
to the sun

4
I am the one without a name
turn, turn again
a tomb, a riddle
a dusky ornament to all
the sea-clocks

5

Curled and crushed
pebble of many blows
drawn and cut
marked by a million tides
the smallest, carrying
one grain of fire from the sun

6

Once I was white
a limb of the white cliff
someone drew a red curtain
over my white skin
someone trod me with
a rusty heel

7

I am a tablet of the writer of sea-memories
the horizon of fish
I am spattered all over with attempts to explain
I move so slowly
trying to fathom the signs
I lie so heavily
I cannot remember my name

QUEEN OF CLAY

for Laura

And my room is red and warm she said
round and warm of the red earth
berries that fell and bled
the snake whose skin is shed
I wear a mask to capture your head
I am white acid she said, she said

The numbers fall tinkling into my lap
the stars ejaculate into my head
a land I outwitted bleeds through my flesh of silk
a house I deserted stretches an evening shadow into my lap
Twelve names, seven summers
the book writes me into itself, humming
I am the small girl, my own child-mother
I cradle my own heart under the sky
she runs into my lap, afraid of thunder
the roar of the heavens, the roar of blood falling
she feels my tears that fall for the earth that is dry
Question the blood and the winter
shall it be stone or a bright new ring
shall it weave corpses into the spring
shall I ride summers with whips or with stars?

And my room is round and blue she said
the blue of an ice-crystal
the shine of an ice-mirror
The child has gone to bed
the mother has turned her head
I am a white page she said, she said

AN INVITATION TO TELL

I am more than an atomic sky, a noiseless particle
a faceless luminosity, a sheath of air
I have a tongue, I pronounce names
I fold my mother gently, paper-thin
into the bottom-drawer
I hold her frail as the moon

I can tell stories, invent my population
The autumn sky carries no ribbons
My child is no blonde innocent
she is capable of hatred, of eclipse

It is all here in the moment's stillness
the war that was a rumour
the entrenchment of faces into their moulds
floral pinafores and the stink of death
a shawl covered with flowers of hoar-frost
scarecrows at the edge of my heart

Dull and dry as a corpse, days of roses
Their faces stare at me like etchings in the wall
railings of light and shadow
music like needles on the leaves of plants

I am more than an equation, sum of memory
I have an unknown pulse to prove it
an anonymous place of pale yellow spring
And I can marry over again
my mother laid in a drawer paper-thin
Is there a name for the second birth?

THE INSECT KITCHEN

Is the clock wound up, is it wound?
he said,
waving his bandaged fist
Round the table he stalked her
his gunmetal head wrapped in linen

You with your jaws, your jaws
you eating up all my words
like a great daft sheep
like a penny machine
like a heifer, she muttered

Has the cat been fed, been fed
with the shreds of supper?
he whispered,
and lapped at her silky legs
and the pipes freezing

You with your centipede heart
and trying to net me
she hissed,
and the milk boiling

Wrap up the tablecloth
and bind my head
Patch up the walls
I'll play knives with you
now all the family's
safe in bed, she said

Is the curtain pulled, is it pulled?
he croaked,
his breath like a sliver of glass,
And the spider shakes in its corner
the webs all alight
the marigolds falling

Five times round the table
his eye rolling, they prance
among the parsley, the petals
the garlic, the ironing-board

Soon her old grey cardigan lay
like a rag on the floor
and her skirt was over her head
as he did the round once more

THE SISTERS

And I made myself a surrogate wedding-day
bought a few scraps of lurex and a tin of salmon
a set of lace mats from the bric-a-brac shop
a feather or two, and a plastic arum lily

> *and she sat in the park where the old house was*
> *where the ruins paved the way to happiness*
> *the last storm had torn a tree through the heart*

The light was thick and keen, the cake shone
I stitched the silver threaded cloth in bunches
on my fat hips and sugared my heavy lips
The radio voice said we may expect thunder

> *and the roses shone like beacons in the dust*
> *and all the window ledges eaten with rust*
> *she picked her way by starlight between stones*

Someone had dropped cherry-juice on the lace
I pinned it to my hair, a creamy ring
of arcane light. Well into the night
I folded tinfoil round two dozen cardboard bells

> *and in the morning, laid like an old maid*
> *upon her work, the new light flickered in vain*
> *She stared among the ruins and the broken cake*
> *The lace fell like swans' feathers over the lake*

FAMILY OUTING – A CELEBRATION

And I took myself for a walk in the woods that day
all ten yards of me, family and all
All of my dear old aunts shuffling in the leaves
and my sister, married now, out on parole
And I took my wives and my daughters, carrying provisions
(in case the sun might hurt) under the green leaves
And my father, with his stern blue eye
and the ancient poodle, gone grey, between us all.
Gran, bringing up the rear, the arch-surrogate
My mother's white shoes flashed in the sun
The luggage that was carried by everyone
would sink a liner, certainly it submerged me.

But the sun was bright, Aunt Alice sprightly
I knew Gran had fresh cucumber sandwiches
tucked in her bag. I told the family not to lag
but keep together, in case of accidents.
We didn't want all of that gnarled old tree
spilling its marrow, for all the world to see.
Sometimes the path vanished beneath the ferns
and father called upon to redirect us all
would puff and blow at all the energy
needed to decide, under the blinding light
of mother's white suit, and equally white
and blinding quality of mind. In the end

He charged in one direction, scattering the aunts
whose china ornaments didn't stand a chance
against such sudden choice; my mother's voice
was heard among the cows three fields away
The family, in sudden disarray, without identity
fell like a pack of cards upon the wind
and needed several minutes of a precise kind to
close ranks against the nosy, scattering breeze.

I picked up Aunt Mathilda's carrier bag and mittens
and Gran's clean pressed linen handkerchieves
dusted the loose earth from Doris's floral dress
and rescued Uncle Jack from the carpet of damp leaves.

The path was narrowing now, and cheek by jowl
we squeezed beneath the nettles and the thorns
clinging together in tottering, whimsical support.
Without a thought, I saw the grisly snarling fangs
of some old beast of prey among the undergrowth
But no-one noticed, only father seemed to dig his heels
harder in the mud, and mother's brand-new suit
was stained with grass and tea from her reluctant tasks
and all the flying insects in their mad assault
upon her, as she shone forth like an old bronze mask.
I should have worn my plastic mac, she said
and Jack said, here's mine, you only have to ask.

Gran was guardian of that particular roundabout
Her iron will pressed down upon the nearest bough
which burst to let the assorted family through.
The shadow of no name was snapping at her heels
as every night he prowled the brown linoleum
of Gran's dark stair, and caught me watching there
under the raven moon, the starless careful night.
I wished the poppies and the cornflower blue
of father's eyes, and mother's clean white lawns.
And soon the ancient poodle fell down dead
and mother wept as though it had been him
My father's arms and legs were very thin.

It seemed the passing of that canine life
unpicked the seams holding the party fast
And so the great disaster came at last
letting the thunders loose, the pricks and spoils.
Mathilda cut across the fields for home

and vanished in the grasses; tired though he was
my father carried in addition, all of my mother
almost smothering her; and Gran, though strong
began a winding down of her most constant song.
To cut a story short (by almost half a life)
they fell like harvest-corn, long over-ripe
into their caverns, into their haunted rooms,

Leaving mine empty, the clean scythe in my hands.

DRESSING-ROOMS

He wears the banners of freedom
as he whistles to work
his fiery bicycle, his keen eye
and the grainy landscape opening
to his feet, to memory

She wears the white flags
printed with hands
The horizon shimmers out-of-doors
somewhere the threshold promising
a kind of straw-bargain

She tries to dress him
in the underworld, his wool socks
without names, his coat for good weather
In peacock shirts, catching fire
along the brimming street

He dresses her in white or black
according to fortune. He buys
blouses by the hundred for her future
stroking the cloth-bales in passing
fingers her hems, folds the collars down

When he undresses
she smoothes the cloth to silence
shedding the rough hours
and he takes her skirts
to bed, closing in
on the elusive texture
of her day's visitors

BIRD

I wasn't at all sure it was a pigeon
when it broke the air.
Its sudden flutter split the bright day
to its root. A shaft of dark
sent its spearhead across this paved space
cursing the children.

I wasn't at all sure
and the bird came large, and occupied
the page, my storehouse of disaster.
It was a long time before
the scattered feathers settled
and I could take myself to
the butcher's shop, where I have learned
a thing or two; the price of meat
and the meaning of hide instead of feathers;

As though this bird-breath had invaded
the world of stone, axe and carcass.

CONSERVATORY FOR LADIES OF PLEASURE

I keep my orange in a glass house,
the hot wet leaves breathing against its skin.

I keep my blue dress in the refrigerator,
soon a constellation of silver needles on the sleeves.

I keep my first ring on a high shelf,
the wind poked a finger through it, a love-draught.

I keep my handkerchief in a shallow grave,
the heavy earth holds its life steady.

I keep my shoes up under the eaves,
to borrow from the chemistry of roofs.

I keep myself in a glass conservatory,
among the orange groves, breathing tropical dreams.

VOCABULARIES

First I attempt to wrap it
in stout paper, which folds well
and regulation string
allowing only a brief flight
on the label, where I drew a bird
absently, as though it flew
by accident in at the window

Then I copy it, row by row
into my stern black books
with a velvety black pen
over and over, converted into
new currency, my profit and
my loss, the time-table
Each line marches in my bones

Then I take to walking
past it, the room upstairs
heavy with untapped messages
the kitchen veiled, and I sing
to rival it, as I march
marshalling each room, inspecting
the forces of print, machine and flesh

For my body hums in it
like a radio set turned down
a tiny wire alive in the corner
and the green tuning-eye that glows
like a cat. I lick my paws
and stroke the ruffled skin
Silence is cracked by its own name

LOOSE ENDS

He covered her hair. It shone too bright and made his days dazzle.
He took her red shoes and locked them in a stout box.
He erased her name from their shared furnitures, and left
his own scent on the cushions and the light-switches.

Then he left the house. It was good that the road was wide
without neighbours. His travelling companions moved like shadows
beyond the shores of that smooth, enclosed ice-river. Surely
he could tread the stone of this fine free highway forever?

For the birds sang, and his legs swung one
after the other. He could have a fathomless lover
who would wait like a deep well he could sing into; she
would not squeeze him like a bellows, or borrow the back of him.

So the fields arched and promised. He came to a river; he came
to a house and his indestructible bone-self frayed at the edge.
In the café, a woman came to serve him, who wore red shoes,
who disturbed with her word the dense earth where he had
                                                    buried her.

THE MEETING

He opened the car door. There was a low rumble
which could have been my heart or could have been
the engine breathing. Or could have been the
distant thrust of a lorry bringing supplies to the
end of England. He stood holding the door.
I stood and listened to unimaginable insects in the
nearby grass and rolled my warmness among the stems
and blades and fragrances. I walked the ten paces
to the car. Inside was hot and fierce. It was
summer.

He opened the car door and his arms flung wide
like great wings of a preying bird. It seemed he
wore an opaque and unusually vivid shirt which
clamoured for attention like market stalls and
birdwings. The trousers were grey and soft like a
mole. I liked his menagerie. The hills opened.
I praised the grand opening bars of this sonata lost
among west country lanes. The threads of such a
morning were held in a tight skein. Later I could
replace my steps while the scarlet upholstery was too
hot like the breath of a stone.

He opened the car door in parenthesis. The event
was of no significance. We met at the station at
three forty-two and exchanged timetables. His hands
lay in his pockets. They only came out to open the
car door. A man and a woman fled across the tarmac
like two refugees from warfare. He entered the car
at the same time as I – perfect parallel lines.
Immaculate guests at a convention, slicing the territory
of love precisely into two halves.

31

He opened the car door and his shirts fell softly
so that I dared not interrupt them. There is no
interfering with falling stars. In the dying season
he was grey and camouflaged. No soldier and no gun.
Only a fallen woman he mourned for. So I crept to
the car and squeezed past the ghost who guarded the
door. The one who looked out of his eyes.

He opened the car door, his face written with many
births and the folds of departures. Between one
moment and the next, a bridge built and bombed. The
world fought and died in its jungle, while we read
the several histories calligraphed in a diminutive
hand on the metal door-frame. The life not yet
invented.

CLAY-SPARROW, DREAM-HAWK

The bird is tight in its pack of loam.
Seawards earth leans, dissolving.
His claw prints mud, his beak utters
the gravel of egg splintering.

He gobbles, the mud is written.
He pecks, the names are seed.
He's a fossil-bird leased from memory
squawking his greed.

Oh my companion you eat too much
my fingers, my neck, my dress-collar.
Now you begin on my heart
you are too far in altogether.

Print-bird of the ancient mudflats
song-bird of an impossible flight
I will introduce you to one another
talk, talk through the greedy night.

Bird risen from the roar of dream
to this raw mating of hand and feather
stay wild yet dumb at the mouth of the cave
or I am made woman and bird together.

WE ARE BOTH DIFFERENT

We are both different
and the same
And that is why we can
go round and round again

You are my next of kin.
Or are you the master who rules
our distances, or the slave binding?

You turn in your sleep
and the fixed stars catapult
from orbit, to eternity.

You smooth a stray hair
and I am alight in such shadow
though my bones weep.

Keep us all within the ring
of names, to each his calligraphy.
Our hands dissolve into applause

for your night-dancing
the owl in daylight.
One more song, and we'll know you.

FISH OUT OF WATER

In this house laughter emigrates
into a corner, worries the dust.
Yesterday they drove bores
into the mountain, fingers of iron
muscles of the forest.

We are too high above sea-level
not a sound from such altitudes.
We wait like carrion for the word.

A sheep's skull, dead eye of the hill
and the house folds round it.
To enter here is to feel the great
magnet earth claim its population.

Elsewhere men occupy the power-station
and the war-head. The rest of us
try for our houses in the mute wood.

UN-FAIRYTALE

After the wedding, frog leapt
    gladly back into his skin.
The mirror splintered when no face
    of hers shone there.
The lady of sighs let down her
    long gold hair
And waited, as the centuries
    crept past her window.
The princess and her prince slept
    unmolested by fruit.
Giant grins like an early
    species of baboon
Spitting his curses playfully
    from the clouds like pips.
A splinter in the bridegroom's
    heart was a mother's
Vengeance, and was not sent by
    the fleshless snow-queen
On her way north, that's a dead story.

They all rise up again
    miming and flickering
That dream army where the child
    once guessed the
Trick, that all was for sleep.
    And waking is like
A pond's split surface, like
    the skin her love
Creates for her now when he touches
    it, and she opens
And arranges herself, not at all
    tidily, into the story.

OCCUPATIONAL HAZARDS

Each time I turn towards the palace, a voice
at the other end of the line tells me helicopters
are extinct.

Each time I clean the sink of fingerprints, I
am a blood-donor, blueprint for the pale fish.

Each time the cat bites, I am reminded that
even a queen must kill.

Each time mama-doll howls, I bandage my daughter's
wound with rose-petals, stitch on an arm.

Each time I wind the clock, my father measures
sand through his toes, a life-timer.

Each time a wave crests, there are fallen
angels, requiem of the water-fly.

Each time a bullet slices life from its root,
I am less than my brother, more than my word.

SHIP OUT OF WATER

Or How The Tailor Cuts Our Cloth
(for Geriatric Critics)

There's time, he said, for improvement
in middle-age she's only just begun
but if she tries she'll make it by the time she's
sixty, if she watches how the Martians get it done.

His day a needle's eye, through it a world gone
lean, skimpy you'd almost say, this cloth won't
meet across our flesh, the cut's too mean.

We're squeezed like hothouse lemons to oil
this tailor's meal, sharpen his fibrous tongue.
Our histories need stitches, so he thinks
our songs the blasphemy of seams undone.

An early death confines him to his chair.
From there he ticks and tracks, and marks
the errant march of hair and thread
across a page, under his itchy scissors blade

while we dare new disguises, kiss of
a claw, lair of the uninvented shade.

DOCTOR FRANKENSTEIN LOSES THE KEY

So he turned into the tomb
wiping the rock-sweat with his new white gloves.
There were stalactites to tickle him
and the rock–flowers that pierced his shoes.

Surely he did not mistake the rendez-vous?
The curious silence and the dripping rock
deafened his question. It's all a matter of
time, he said, and the cave swung in the hands
of a great wind, flung to the far edge.

He made patterns in the hours. As he waited
the picture-books defied his calendars.
One snail spun longer than his day.
The game outwitted him.
The tomb sacrificed its heart.

AUNT GLADYS

She doesn't approve of kissing in public.
She clicks her tongue at the bus-stop
at his hand promising the girl's bowed spine.
She sends back catalogues when they display
forests of peach and avocado underwear
and crosses the street where the soft-porn shop
sits at the pavement's fork, window of discreet
frilled cavities in cloth, slits in the lace.

Her face leans earthwards.
Her mouth is a soft fall of skin
away from its tongue.
She closes it tight as a back door
against burglary
or the footfall of a priest
or the wide arms of a nagging memory.

At night the cat fondles her.
She dreams of a man whose mouth
never crossed the threshold
moistening her
whose lips spoke in their turn
whose only occupation is the glazed and
burnished frame of guilt where she has
banished him, brother to the prayer-plant
and a single line of prose punched out
one august as his blood sprayed patterns
on some foreign earth, her name once only
reaching for the stars.

WINKLING

The chalk cliff sends back light
does not take us in like the warm red clay
of Devon, these bone-cliffs of Sussex
pushing us back.

At the cliff's foot my father's legs are white
straddling the rock.
He's rolled his trousers tight over the knee
and calls me over the stones and pools
waving his net.

Beneath the water-surface, green-laced silences.
A dumb mouthing creature, plankton
and pale fish.

We wield our transparencies,
his arm a beam solid as the structure
of this one day leaping like a shrimp.

Picking the pale flesh out of its stone,
curling it out of its pearl corridor
we taste much later
the belly of the sea.

ELSIE'S REVERIE

On Sundays, hunting the shore
Elsie caresses the trousers she wore
and feels the warmth of deep pockets
nibble her fingers' ends.

She probes the pools and wishes
green algae into the garden
of her head.

George was as good as dead
and she combed the beach alone
for winkles and rock-creatures
trailing her daughters.

They are draped with weed
like dressmakers' scraps.

They'll not haunt her
these small and smaller versions
of a coutured self.
Only George the unforgiven
pops up in the land of chalk
pointing out a pathway
among the rock-islands
his white shirt flapping.

Honey melts on the shelf.
Time eases through her room.
Love wriggles in its sack
like a trapped poacher caught
under eaves, daring too much.

OCCUPATIONS

One

My sickle child
she's a moon ahead of me

under the lip of the hill
practising how she'll
leap the archipelago
into the light

She's made of ice as yet
or raw blood
a bunch of fibres
tissue red and white

I've a box, a room
a hollow lined
with something like magenta
colours rich as dark
to host her in

She swims my eye's avenues
lithe as a minnow
her futures swiftly turning
between other fish

deft as an unearthed
thought, and fathomless

Two

There's a shape
that was made for me
for future tenancy

Once a box, its corners
glared like teeth
shouldering out to the four
corners of the earth

a sharp reminder of
definition
getting your angles right
and brisk persuasion

Now it's a stone's mouth
a bone's leaning
a supple space pouching
its fish
soft as the springing arch
of bone I once tore through

An edge gone lame
a corner clipped
face in the chip of stone

The marching columns
ease into untidy camp
my limbs' belongings
scatter over the valley
a rampant lichen
creeper and tumbleweed

and the rocks have a new green skin
mossing their cleft

Three

He's a presence among the leaves
of jasmin, of old oak

He's a footprint
dovetailed into mine
beneath the heel

He's a cloud of pollen
on the run
a hive of cotton-threads
weaving his cloth

Sun does not penetrate
his vein
nor drum his ear

I dream him lustily
my tide rears him and
throws him back

Somewhere between the wave's
crest and falling
this fish escapes

HER PENTHOUSE OF RARE LOVE

Orange walls that glare like a sun
too fierce, always noon, and its shadow of
peach-powder like ash on all the surfaces.

Her fingerprints break that web
here and there, and an old shoe
tarnished and grounded for good
grumbles in the spidery corner
not bright enough for rescue.

This is the room of a queen.
The curtains say so with thick
arpeggios; the bedspread
proclaims it, crater of love
and no gravity.

The walls are witnesses, her swanning
song over Venetian bridges
microcosm in a gondola
and the stiff staircase of frills
budding on a petticoat, made
for fiesta in a scorpion heat.

The spare, dead days.
Her rooms buzzing with flakes
of shed-skin, a universe
of urns; only the photographs
glow in a cabinet, rich as monstrance
approached with a careful fingering
as though bones might shred also into dust.

Once in a while she wakes too early
and the sky is paling then with promises
of splendour. Her gowns hang
like sleeping bats, they have
their own transmitters.

Then the new day cracks her open.
Below milk-bottles, clinking of
castanets in a distant land.

SOMETIMES LOVE

Sometimes loving is a claw in the desert, machinery
of shells, looking for a promise of water.

Sometimes loving is the word that freezes a man
and a woman forever, joined at the root.

Sometimes loving is too near, like bright
beetles through the eye of a snake.

Sometimes loving is hot and presses hard on the
heart, a cat-burglar, of no fixed address.

Sometimes loving is a room too full of voices,
as though all channels came to a head.

Sometimes loving is the footfall unforeseen, the
quiet shifting of one day's ashes.

Sometimes loving speaks like a foreigner and the
sound is like a subterranean tournament.

Sometimes loving is an arrangement of chairs, the
judge's leather and dark velvet for drowning in.

Sometimes loving falls off the edge of the page
into fingers and hands that cannot speak of it.

THE THIRD WOMAN

One was sleek and white and curled
round his legs on a Sunday night
and cupped his twisty heart like a twin
to her own, to put her loving in.

Two was tall and measured him up
for her days of marching round the loving-cup.
She sliced and boned and slit and scored
and kept his heart in a cupboard stored.

Three was black and three was red
three was a witch beneath the bed.
Sometimes a saint, sometimes a whore
singing in his bones for evermore.

PLAYING FOR TIME

She curled like a shell around the instrument
borrowed from the earth.
Then arranged her sisters, note by life.

Each note struck lens, glass, boot
the stricken sun, a yellow star.
Each note cast ribbons in her hair
painted the beloved name she wore
unbroken.

The commanders sit
enraptured, in the lap of victory
stroking their taut wings of prey
eased by thin lips
that parted like a bell.

She swung them, paragons of order
into the soft heart of France
and all her bones sprung like the violin
of her sister, playing for time.

One wore grey and one wore black.
One wore flesh like a loose cloak.
The other measured it inch by inch
across the bone, hour by hour.

Across the mud-village
smoke curls like sweet songs from tall windows.
Her sister went gladly to the tin rose
that might succour her, that
spilled the black rivers of her future
smiling as she offered flesh and name
to paradise, beyond the smoke.

The concerto billowed as she choked
on nothing but a name, on the great hordes
on lies, and heard her sister
pronounce sentence on the death orchestra.

They kept her boots with all the others
marching silently in the rag parade
seizing the dust, clung like a lover.
It was Venice, the Polish pavilion
thirty years on.
Violin across the lagoon
madame butterfly roasted to a stick.

Note: Fania Fanelon is a French Cabaret singer and Alma Rose the niece of
Gustav Mahler. In the death camps of World War II, certain prisoners' lives were
saved by the fact that they had musical ability. They joined the camp orchestra
and were required to sing or play for their captors.

THIS TIME

This is a wry time, a spy time, movement of ship
and hand across distant oceans, our land
pock-marked with a few signals from the deep well.

Oh yes, we're well, our medical services second
to none, our nurses have their caps in place, the sun
will always come again from behind obedient houses.

Put your house in order, they say. I have a few new
cushions, cover the cracked paint with a second skin
and watch the rebel wall spread its bouquet of rank flowers.

For there's a hospital ship and our boys are first-class
and there's something alien about the Argentinians
as though they wore scales or too much hair on their thighs.

And pink and English men of the fair flesh, our grey boys
carnivores in shiny suits, rubbing their itchy backs against
the Dover cliff, keeping the road to paradise intact.

I'm well, my food is good, I have a colour set, and
the new season is fingering my sunny orange dress, yet
as Stevie said, in spite of smiles, someone is drowning.

SEAHOUSE

for Enid

The sea sings in its core of flesh
a fine bone flute
a spine of ringing vertebrae
small measure of tides strung through her ears
like invisible shells coiling the water
into cones of fish-sound
the breeding heart of time plotting its next move
inchwards up the cliff
each stroke of the sea's edge
a signature.

A maimed and limpid day
the habitation of starfish
trailing torn weed among the wrecks
sea nosing among the bones
leaking its silt.

Her head turns blindly
towards its kingdom
fish-lights speckle her eyes.
Her skull aches with the weight
of ocean.
They'll need to drain her to
the sea-bed
for her breast-bone
the crusted fingers of her crab-life
where she sings rusty.

LOVE TO A CAREFUL HAND

Hand, you were once a sudden lance of flesh
over a waterfall, the books cascading
into your trap.
You were too slippery for arm's length
off upriver to a new spawning-ground
riding the obstacle of words tumbling
like an avalanche, too many of them
trying to hold you back.

Now I beat you to it, he's a prize catch.
I found him out with teeth
with plasm and my legs spread like Atlas
over his kingdom.

Hand you're too late
too slow
much used to tracing with your index
and filling in of gaps.

Now you're a trailing weed of fingers
afterword of water where its run
last at the touch, still trying to translate
your late discovery
into the safe and closed fist of a dictionary.

UNMINDFUL

At six o'clock I turned on the television
to watch the six o'clock news
and to my surprise there appeared in full colour
a picture of Mount Olympus, and the gods
arrayed in all their splendour one above the other.
Then I saw that Zeus was looking a little peculiar.
He'd obviously had a sex-change or liked
dressing up as a woman. His wreath of golden laurel
looked curiously like a dried and frizzy wig
and why was he dressed in a blue suit and a false bosom
waddling across a bleak street and not
enshrined on his mountain. And why did he stand
in the posture of a warrior, but the words coming out
fell like chips of wood and clattered on the steps
of Downing Street. I did not understand.
Zeus seemed somehow to have slipped out of his clothes
and gone walk-about. You can see warts
on his chin and his Olympian team
look all the same. Their spears must be hidden
in those oblong black slabs they carry in their hands
and the sky wears a flat white veil like a shroud.
So I decide to write a letter to the gods
and send it care of the British Broadcasting Corporation
in case the camera had a warp in the lens
or perhaps my set wants tuning, or I've put
my contact lenses into the wrong eyes
and the world's turned upside-down. Perhaps that
hole in the road is Olympus in reverse
and Zeus is lying at the bottom of a well
his voice a long way off, so all you hear
is the faintest echo of what a man or woman
(who can tell which is which) might once have been.

GETTING THERE

I couldn't remember the name of the band
or the pub, or the man I am supposed to love,
stepping out on Saturday against the black wall
of the London road at night, only a slight
tug at the umbilical when we passed the pet-shop
where we'd found baskets, flaps and collars –
clever confinements for our regressive cat.
And I remembered my husband's lean hand
calming the fur, as I lay all riddled,
shrunken after a journey; and how the house
settled like a cloak on me and had me back –
masked it's true, but then our skin defies
disguises and small indulgencies poke through.

Passing the darkened pet-shop and the laundry
memory didn't know its place, pierced pin-holes
in the bland sheet-lighting of the London road
as though someone shoved a hot thin needle
in my breast and pulled it out again, so fast
the quick sting had no time for recognition.
We leaned against the wind and found the venue
beyond the Co-op, undertakers and the Oxfam shop.
A man with a squeeze-box and an eager beard
whisked the air a little with his songs
that didn't stretch into our fidgety laps
but fell like tired birds wounded in the nest.
Then the band came on, swept up the dead
and turned our sleeping genius inside out.
I always wanted skinny arms, a body hanging
lank and white inside a bleached vest, as though
all colour leapt to her head; the fiddler worked
her bow, as I do late at night when the moon teases
you to death, your linen shining like the ice-cap,
a great white eye that's almost fit to blind you.
Sylvia is here, and Laura glowing in her self-embrace
arms hooked on each other for neither love nor money,

caging a fancy shirt that beams its pattern out
to keep her heart from too close dance, too early.

A hand-rolled cigarette gleams on the wood
next to my glass; Sylvia's wearing Jasper Conran,
a mine of silver at the neck, falling like ransom.
And yet her bush of hair curls like tobacco.
I hold this thin cigarette as a rare purchase,
light it up, knowing the rasp and kick of where
we came from and where we might be going.
Smoke across the fiddler's bones, her arching throat.

CATCH

I woke up in the middle of the night
on Wednesday the eleventh of October
in the small hours, when blackness sinks
low in the belly and your ears are like
bright steel rods that wave in the room for clues.
And I heard this sound between my legs
in the wild land there, that was never husbanded,
land left to graze and scattered with small scrub bushes.
As I listened, it seemed that many tiny fists
were beating on my inner walls
hammering with their soft knuckles on the slithery
passages I've learned to blaze and also
to be wary of; so hearing that gathering population
thunder in there, as though storm brooded
way off over the Beacon, where night is a little
madder than I am, a little redder at the rim,
I know that my children call to me from their cells
fisting for life, angry and dumb with their fish-mouths
not to be carved by the good air, into human.
My children call, all the red patches in the room
seem lit, as though a lamp switched on
which shows only red – the poppy stitched
on a tapestry cushion, the scarlet wax run loose,
my shoe, my shoe tilted heavenwards,
all glowing in the night's burn-out, completed.
My eyes are fearful of these finished things
clamouring their craft. I say to all my lost ones,
love, hard to believe, and harder still to catch
allowed you out – too soon, too soon upon the
world's clasp, you had no tools to swim with.
I say to them, I love you still, my fish, my unborn warriors.

AVOCADO

He left an avocado in the fridge
I took it out and held it, felt it plump and soft
carried the coffin out of last night's dream
and ate the pear he left behind; then roamed the bleak forest
like a randy goat, there where our winter ghosts are out.

I ate the avocado my husband left me
and took to the loose woods with a perfect vagabond
hugged in my last year's scarf, biting the wind's ice
out in the new-made raw, half-in half-out of dream
the day that never quite launched itself into the light.

We kept our fists hard-balled in worthy jackets
and I am used to fencing with the dark so snipe and
circle through the bare trunks skinned of last year.
The sky presses down, and so we tramp. I have you
in my eye's pocket where the flotsam gathers
deep in the seam. I have you where you tell me
that your house bears old lace, cinnamon, the wide-eyed
island where you grew; and I could marry you
were it not for all that dead wood.

As for me I believe I lodge in the crevice of your root
between my clever angles, where the woods slide
out of sight, eased like that coffin in my dream
last night, we carried back, back to the old worn room
we fell from. There, we said to the assorted family
there is the glowing box its coals alight; see how we
carry it this far and merrily, see how our hands clasp
over the split fruit, green and ripe.

DON'T LOOK NOW

Don't look now
the door is opening on a tête-à-tête
fine wire between the parties
her foot one step upon his flight
he leaning like an angel in a bright shirt
tugging at their cord.

Don't look now
as though to say come on (he says)
playing with light
(and don't attend the company)
time splintering at his neck
her hands there ache.

Don't look, don't look
the crack between the door's extension
and its close, is large enough.
She's caught there on the phone
watching the slit
and don't, the world parts so
its yawn erupting from the mouth
and billowing gaunt and toothless
down the line to take her daughter
(what, what is it, do speak soon)
and then the wild world's lap.

Soon and still soon his flesh, the
valley and the meal are hurly-burlied
round the walls cutting their proofs.
The house flies apart, don't look.
National Geographics fly from the attic
the pavement's spattered with aduki beans
and they lie in each sparse bed jammed
in the door's foot, wondering how
a casual visitor could reap such harvest.

All fall down the nursery says
the child wills it, the pincer-grip
of pain; the need to have the
whole lot out and grinning.

Don't look now
blood and red wine, the spilled country
mock-cavity walls, light splicing through
the lie of what is seen freeze-frame
and out of joint; her hero mangled
in the twinkling of an eye.

TIGER

In the corner an old sailor is dreaming of tigers
in red weather. She would like to open his face
and let them out. She knew once what it meant to
be tiger, how you could crouch low on the ground,
fierce and ready.

It was a long time ago.

In the corner an old sailor is dreaming of the heart
of darkness, is dreaming of where the path mates with
jungle, is dreaming of land pitched against him, and
how the sky was bloody with torn hide.

His eyes fold back.

She watches the sailor dreaming in the corner in
red weather, flare of a flower-head out of the green
thick as lava.

The jungle boils.

She has never been to the jungle. She would not
survive there. Her feet are not hard for tracking.
She'd sniff her own death too near, always
approaching.

What does it mean to be like him, an old sailor
dreaming of tigers. You watch and remember the
animals under the stair. The lair of dream, the
way something catches you out ready to pounce even
now. Is it called tiger? Does it belong to
sailors?

In the corner an old man meeting his beasts. Perhaps his hand clenches now sniffing the darkness, feeling the animal near. Perhaps he is conjuring all the crouching jungle in his pale eye.

In the corner she writes of an old man. Her coat is red. Tiger is dream, is a word in her book. He crouches ready to meet whoever will conjure him.

AFRICAS

This doll beats his drum.
If this doll came of grass he would
tramp the field down.
But he is root-crop, blade-hidden.

If this doll asks, how shall I answer?
He makes time curl out of his belly
like a dark snake.

If I ask this doll, how is his tongue made
will it have time to spell the hours
of his dancing, before the scythe dips?
Which time will he choose for his saying?

This doll beats her drum.
The sound is locked in.
Shall I ask of her land a different
colour, a basin of dreams.

She thrusts out her breasts and speaks.
How are they carved, parted across
the table, how are they twin.

OPENING THE RIVER

Today I am woman coming to the edge of water
to wash linen caked with dust. How the air resists
my thighs, pushing through. How water clasps me
blue at the foot, white froth on my raking hand.

I haven't been here before, this bowl of water.
The trees are talking thin today. I don't know
how the rinsing water is dissolving threads,
my legs are water-quiet, pitched against flood.

Lifting like sacrifice, the basket creaks wide with sun
its clothes stiffened with earth, their spines crack.
Water sparking out of clay, my shoulder is a bending
hollow; when I enter, river holds there smiling.

NEWS FROM THE BRIGHTON FRONT

The man takes a stone.
He grunts. A chip flies from its flank.
He mixes metaphors.
It winks blue and purple under the crazy pier.

The woman takes a stone.
Its blue skin is startled by her scarlet nail.
She traces a name in its cool fist.
The letter grumbles on her bag's seabed.

Between her feet, sea gnashes, her silver heel
knocks on wood. Waterskin catches her face,
throws it back. Only fish have tunnel vision.
She strolls the pier tossing her hooks overboard.

Honeyman eating candyfloss in a blue striped
blazer. Honeyman in a check suit that yells
summer. Honeyman with nothing in his pockets,
tilted like a liner, waving to the fat thighs
with a pale unburned hand.

You are all used up, she tells the fruit-machine.
Orange peel shredded from the sun's fracture.
Man under the pier tied up with string. Sun
sticking his limbs together. Soon his face will
shine out of its bag, thirsty for fruit.

The woman sees that he is thirsty.
She asks him the time. A watchface spins
in his eye's cyclone. I never stay long
enough, he says.
An hour crawls between her legs. She leaves
him straddled on the weedy groyne.

Going hunting. The crazy pierstakes.
Hunting a crack in the day. Through which
he may pour fish-oil and sweat and the voice
of a romping sea.
Going hunting. Trying to escape from his
string vest. Looking for tunnels into the
light. Her skirts up round the motorway.
It winks blue as a stone.

The man is selling monkeys. Their felt jackets
shout at the strollers like parakeets. Pavements
hot as a jungle. The monkeys chatter, wondering
at the origin of species. Ice-cream runs from
their mouths like the tongues of lilies.
Summer spilling.

The sea wakes first, a thin silver needle.
Then the man breathes earth in through paper
shoes. On the promenade, in the white hotel,
she wakes next in her ruffled bed.
Her sheets itch.

At coffee time she sits in her deckchair
reading the penguin book of contemporary
beetroot recipes.

I've reached rock-bottom she tells her friend,
he's gone back to his wife. The gull flies
too high screaming in ecstasy. He has the
wings for it.

Another fish says her friend, another
pale face coming up out of the tank.
What kind do you want in this aquarium,
dogfish or razoreel. They swim the
promenade, noses against glass.

Who needs a Martian eye. Or uncut videos.
Behind the roasting knuckle, each sunbather
preserves an inwardness of palm. Where the
world tickles in.

The Grand Hotel is missing a couple of floors,
a gash in its proud flank.
Sightseers along the promenade, missing a
couple of floors.
Between the death and the death, a lift-shaft
of silence.
Nostalgic rubble hastily shuffles into
the gap.

Boadicea rides again. Roll up!
Her warship cleaves the tired seafront air. The
papers drum up an audience, slot another cylinder
into the penny machine. Cheap at the price.
And the land has a hole in its flank and water
in her leaky shoes.

Marks and Spencers rise to the occasion. Fly a
drip-dry flag. At seven am he pats the pocket
of his silk pyjamas. No credit card. Still the
shirts fly from cellophane to comfort him and
blouses drift across well-heeled breasts to
comfort him.
We do not hesitate to clothe our leaders, says
the manager, unlocking his plate-glass doors
two hours early.

Money down the drain, down the penny-machine,
pouring from the till.
Someone reverses the video and Marks and Spencers
clothes the cabinet. Consolation for a hole in
the side.
We are glad the emperor has a new suit of clothes
says the manager, stroking his assets and his
salesgirl with a shot-silk paw.

She has a hole in her bag where the letter falls
through and her boss pays for the orchestra to play
her evening wide, and the hole in the white hotel
says the critic is where the sightseers crowd on in,
too many of them, the ship splits a seam and begins
its slow march to the sea-bed.

Do not go naked into the conference chamber,
clothe the cabinet of curiosities, speciality
of Brighton, the museum preserves a discrete
shade.

Moving towards winter. Beginning to gather, tanks
on the pierhead in spite of clement weather.
Woman in indian summer deckchairs reading of penguins.
Behind her the Grand Hotel with a hole in its face.
Behind her Boadicea with a hole in her heart. Behind
her the president, a hole in his celluloid.

I don't like this movie, he says, there's a frame
missing where the people ought to be.
Someone left the Indians on the cutting-room
floor.

Behind her the Grand Hotel where leaders danced
waving their gilt-edged securities. Someone said
they're the guardians of the British way of life.
Which is also to say brutal wish to lacerate, or
bomb with love, or even best writers of lies.
She prefers boastful witnesses of limpets, having
one stuck to her shoe. And writes it.

Graffiti under the pier. They're surprised when
the shadows speak, these leaders, it interrupts
the pantomime. Thought Indians were extinct, won't
they ever learn, we're in charge of the cutting-room
floor.

Stone-scratchers that rise up against the town's
cataract and cut its blind face.
It takes an operation to remove a root.

In charge of summer, winter, and in charge of
words for it. The postcard flies in the teeth
of the ice-cap on the other side.
Though her skin's still seasonal.
It hits the president on the chin. He swats
a fly.

In Gatsby-under-Wold he leans to adjust the silver
nipple of his radio set. In Brighton she stretches
to turn down the volume of fish-sound that keeps
escaping from aquariums.
Between them, a continent rises. They give each
other credit for not creating it.
Decide not to consult over the means of exploration.

In the early hours of friday october twelve nineteen
eighty-four, gulls scatter. She wakes in her bed
at two forty-five and asks him if he's locked the
car. The timer creeps to zero, the end of dialogue.
The prime minister leaves the bathroom and launders
her speech. You can smell salt in the backstreets.
He and she fuck across the distances.
They say the fuse was set a century ago.

MATANZAS IN THE BATH ARMS

I'm sitting in the amber shadows of the Bath Arms
the window behind me yellow, wrinkled like ancient skin
and my beer sparking the sun's light deep in its vat.
During that lunchtime stroll to the bar and back
I've tipped over the edge of today's fortress,
swung on my own rope across the moat and landed
in front of him, my hand held out for blessing.
It didn't take long for conversation to prickle
into life; the barman clears my ashtray every time
I twist an empty crisp-packet into a pig's tail
catching the slow whirl of alcohol across the brain
from one ear to another; then the pub's pantomime,
how they drift and posture, how the mid-day punters
sink a pint. Collars shift uneasy on their necks
among the niggle and spite of this one hour's grace.
And the girls together lean on each other's eyes
for confirmation. The barman hovers, executes careful
ballets according to my progress down the glass.
And on the third day he arabesques across my tracks
bloodless spectacles slipping a touch on the bridge
and tells me of Majorca, the flat he owns there
close to the shore, and the high citadel where Chopin
lingered on the terrace, spilled his exquisite notes
to catch the moment's ache between one deepening
indigo and another; I tell him I was there once
on that same hiatus, trying to forge a sensibility
outside my father's frame. He talks of ritual,
the pig they slaughter, slitting the throat
the hulk up-ended to drip his passion out.
And into the Bath Arms steals another music
of the dying beast, his frantic eye, blood pouring
scarlet seams across the carpet and its unlit faces.
The barman turns to sepia, mouthing his tale.
They call it *matanzas*, he says, *matanzas* when he dies.
I hear the scorched earth hissing beneath the pig,

shriek of a vessel loosing its life too fast.

Matanzas, he says, pulling the pump, a golden liquid
spouting merrily from his hand, caught in my glass.

REDUCING THE DOSE

Sometimes the air alone is enough to send
you flying, as though someone split the fruit
and spat you out, a gnarled old peachstone
rattling across salty seafront paving-stones;
no destination. The pier's an arm of oil and glitz
all its wares thrust and bursting out of booths,
kiss-me-quick, prize-every-time stall holders promising,
promising just like the barmaid in the Bath Arms
who's spilt her bosom into the counter's froth of beer
and dangles there, sending you silly with the memory
of home, more push-and-shove back there than all this
box of tricks, a seafront shattering its glassy hold.
And you've been wrapped for decades in soft flesh
staying tucked-up and dreaming in that cave, like Plato
witnessing the shadow-play of limbs juggling their
chances and mouths pronouncing futures you can't catch.

Last night I sliced a quarter of him off
working precisely with the kitchen knife,
knife-point chipping at this minute bomb of blue
as though I'm sorting through old clothes to see
what fits – discard the comforter, the fleecy bodice
and the belt; a pale-blue powder falls and dies there
in the saucer. My blade has taken him for less
and when we twist in love, a quarter-section of me
disconnects and rises from its cramp into fierce air
(the benediction) carrying me like a riddled stone
to the water's edge; a brain, a walnut newly-shelled,
its surface cavernous and lodging in the shingle
or any damned place where the world's blasphemy
erupts into your ear and strangers offer up their gap-tooth smiles.

FAREWELL TO BRIGHTON

All that shingle ringing against its mate
and the sea overlapping into her thighs' fork.
She cases the pier, left behind when dawn creaks in
and celebration dries like an old prune
nobody's choice of breakfast.

And all the landladies close their doors
in a ricochet along the front
saying no, no, in a great chorus of squawks.
The parrots bite her fingers saying 'pretty'.

It is a long time, the pier was always thus
never without its damp undertow
a great fall-down from that bright stair
to paradise, a ruff of pink at the waist
a high white shoe; all tumbled, scuffed
and wanton in the bleary drift of moon
when dawn washes it, the sky scouring
her seafront sutra, her pink net petticoat
awash through all its wires; a long time.

All that shingle; still the stones mutter
against tides, against her heavy dream-swell.

Slowly they leave, the song's belovèd
the one who sang it out; going north or west
leaving the crazy pier, the change machine
the frantic rattle of a seaside town counting its cost.

CONCERNING THE ALLOTMENT

If I think of parsnips it is not to say
I am content with some ordinary vegetable
though the day
my neighbour left that bulbous root
propped against the step without a signature
I must confess the chain reaction
led to you.

I have been more in love with aubergine
a glossy flesh, an obscure bloom.
Eating that hybrid I've a whiff
of old Majorca way above the treeline
and castanets rattling against the ear
the rasp of more exotic fruit
in spite of you.

Going to pot you said, waving your pipe
sending smokerings into the vacant air
and whether vegetables or the nation or
the whole shoot, I can't tell; only cling
to all that architecture we never crafted.

And we never did reach the end of the
garden, the haven of your potting-shed
though travelling the wide lands through
rifling olive-groves and bald high places;
never did make it into husbandry
raking the earth over at the far end
to pull this tuber out.

This vegetable-patch is where
our hidden city crouches in
miniature under the fleshy leaves.

CROSSINGS

for Ernie

Today is silence, not of words' death
although so much is spoken, laboured out.
You lie and fight for each dear minute's
winnings, life's small permission.

You rogue, you've cheated me by going
off like that, out of our circle
taking your war-stories, your warm brown
eye, the sidelong poke at laughter.

My love in the wings waiting to fly.
You won't mind will you if I take off
while you're much more than earthbound
marrying with clay, testing sparse breath.

I'll sing you out dear friend, hold
your knotted hand; and make fire
strong and good. But oh you should have
waited, even now crack in my eager wing.

THE COMPANY SHE KEEPS

for Elsie Lucas

Called up out of the anniversary
the slowly clenching fist your body makes
gracing the marble slab, my voice
carves out the freezing air grandmother
once light as eggshell in your downy bed
now locked and knotted at some final gate
where even I can't knock, can only crouch
afraid and headlong at your foot. I trace
my last lips' track across your forehead
where the road runs into silence; blind
and cold, your bluest eye clamped shut.

Since then I've made you bird again
only to end the flight. I'm dense as winter
in your passing; your voice undoes me when
the sheet falls and my skin's cold glare
tests out its night. I part the curtains
beam you out across the garden's moonstruck stare.
I'm wrapped in absence like the coat you made
me, tucking up the hem; too large, you said
as now this night's undressing, naked stars.

Grandmother light as bird, your threads
that once stitched up my life unravel me.
Bitter on the tongue this day's excess
breathing-in lilac from your apron's cave.

SIMONE DANCES

A quick twitch of silver.
Stars tumble her calf's black stocking.
And he ancient as leather
arches his chest with its pantomime
intact, snaps his braces, launches
his forty years and more
into the lucky space she traces.

Simone dances, her skins
erupt into his ears; lined in black
she drifts a tattered scarf to
bless his scars; his shoulders
wriggle in their middle age.

He croons once more with feeling
an old nerve teasing in his ravished eye.

MUSIC ON VICTORIA STATION

– 18th February 1991

On Victoria station, crossing safely at mid-day,
the crowds of travellers are thrusting harder than usual
against the air, (as though it were thicker
than water and cluttered with obstacles).
In front of me, two tiny busy wheels
support a cello, drawn like a human silhouette
across the pristine floor washed clean of blood.
Her lowered eyes sweep from side to side
like a broom swishing the floor ahead of her
and the cello glides like a privileged guest
across the station, special envoy wrapped in a case,
glides without interrogation through
the mid-day air that cracks like glass,
air that bears invisible splinters and hums
with fear – as though this man here, this one
(carrying his newspaper like a baton)
or that one there, his eyes a shield,
(as though short-sight will cancel everything)
might be your dear protagonist at the last,
that last-ditch stand when light goes out for good
and no more cellos will bell and ache
for you, and no more bows will touch and tease out
sound that rings and worries at your heart.

I follow the woman with that precious hollow
sliding intimate behind, close on her heels,
wanting us both to make it to the overture
as though we have been granted a reprieve,
can start the movement over again, a gift
of one more cello crossing the crowded station.
I am imagining the lift and breach of knees
as she embraces her familiar, while I am
tracking my belovèd in the aftermath, draft
one more day's magnificat in my letter's music
out of the blast and rubble of the southern station.

79

A PROUD SHORE FOR LEGENDS

Well here we are again jumping up and down
upon the shore, eyes all at sea, gobbling
the sand this time (forgetting Malvinas)
dreaming of desert rats, Arabian nights
and all that head-gear. What a year
it's been for camels swaying through our
narrowest needle's-eye. See how our fingers
poke into every pie (greedy before the storm)
into the crack and lull of a sheltering sky,
an inflammation of the digit and the tongue.
And see how the little bastard inside us all
waves his tomahawk, his tommy and his rattle
for our team didn't they, haven't they always won?

★

The boy with a mission polishes his gun
watching planes soar like silk-moths
into that deepening black of where he's
banished cat's-paw touch and raspberry-cane.
For he's American and they have smooth-talked
him and tidied up his plot to put him straight.
All he can do is wait on the shore of sand
securely tarnished. And in his right hand
(silky on the gun) a lifeline leaps and jerks
across the palm then stops before the cleft,
dirt-riddled gulf between his finger and his thumb.

★

They don't tell, don't let on. The screens
of Europe and the USA have made him legend.
At nineteen he's the son of light, a mine
of interference; fuzzy lines upon a grid.
And soon the great lid of the desert-eye will
blink just once and out damned spot he'll go
lancing the wound that never can be bled.
Just like Miss Havisham's wedding captured
in a cobweb before the consummation. No, boy
they'll never marry nor stamp each other out.
But you'll be gone before you know it, and so
the story won't be told you see, the legend.

UNDER COVER

There is a cold place, you will know it.
Not the ice-cap or the tundra
or that cleft in ice where sailors froze
on their haunches, clawing for fish.
Somewhere north, the names escape me
only their skin you can cherish
in the mind's eye, turning blue-white
calling from the back of beyond
where ice gives way, as I do.

Hugging my cardigan round me at
first light, in the place they call
the kitchen, finding water, bread
I know that we travel unexpectedly
my legs quicken with the sudden
flare of you as I part the curtain
though whether you begin at the foot
or sneak your fire across
my tongue, it's hard to tell.

I am boiling water, I know nothing.
You shift yourself to my contours
expertly, no-one would know I carry
more than cups, under the skin
volcanos, meteors, extinguishing
all in the time it takes to remember
dead sailors, light the gas for eggs.

THE MOTHERS

Imagine a town, a southern town
in high summer. Imagine the sweet break
of strawberry on the tongue, at a table
in a café, at the innermost cleft
of one of those street-corners near the sea.

And then imagine the woman,
her daughter poised like a bird across
the table, candles adrift in her eyes,
a starlit birth she can't remember.
It stretches dark and tasting faintly of fruit
beyond the rim of the table, the door's jamb,
the smallholding of their twenty years together.

You cannot imagine, as this frosted birthday-cake
splits on each tongue and juices stain their
twisting lips, how wide the mouth that utters
forth its howl, how another woman's fingers
claw at all that rúbble, just one shoe,
a single leg like stone, the less-than-grown
sweet belly of her black and charcoaled daughter.

The morning after, the English mother, licked through
with strawberries and the night's long limb of sex
lifts a golliwog from the box outside the bric-à-brac shop.
She thinks of marmalade, peeling the golliwogs
among her grandmother's blue and marbled shadows,
picks up the doll and stares at his grinning face.
Just as the ground in Sarajevo gapes again
to swallow black blood and brackish water,
just as the Bosnian mother holds the taste of birth
upon her tongue, just once before her face cracks,
the horizon splits and the belovèd world is cloven.

As though the fault-line runs in memory beyond
all sense, tearing through Bosnia to the seaside town
where the knife eases through sugar, a woman wishing
with the weight of all her futures still intact.

THE WOMAN WHO MISTOOK HER FATHER
FOR AN IRISHMAN

He was an upright man, a too-tight man
a man of honour, a man of blight, a sight
of land, a one-man band, a sweet tobacco
curling in the wool of his all-English coat.

He ruled, he puffed, he parked the car
in twenty jolts and shifts, he lifts the
load, adds up the profit, calculates the loss
and doesn't give a toss for her undoing.

Looking after, she remembers, meant a window-seat
a pleated curtain, knives of bone, a battle won
taut strings, an overview, the one who always knew
the globe's best shape, its politics, its scars.

But when they watched the old films flicker, he
and his daughter, from the old plush seats that creak
with laughter; when Chaplin's tickle inches up
the legs and hits the belly hard and rattles there

and when they buckle into raucous groans
her father toppling headlong from his chair
is no more English than this lilt, this flare
of fiery sound that whips the heart to bits.

Then he's a tramp, a man whose song assaults
the Irish sea with unrequited love, until
the old gods tell him who he is and she can
recognise a rakish eye, a fiddler buried deep

and so far down her father's Irish heart is cleft
and hidden in his tweed, his socks, his tread
the rumbling of his wanton dreams in bed
air's hiss as he draws a breath of music

through his pipe, in the mean time of the year,
the catch of breath flaring his pipe's bowl
like a crucible, nations welded in the ash
his daughter's heart a carbon copy of his own.

NOLI, ECCE

With words I can make a web
where the air will stretch
between us, a fine-fibred wall
too thin to hold, you seep through.
And what I catch are forms of you
the shape of your feet a white
glow beyond their leather, the
frost-bitten brow of your shoulder
moves like lightning, I can
catch it, I am a fine conductor.

And the time is fragrant with
spikenard, now I have tracked it
down the centuries, to the first
man's haunt, his garden, or where
I drew out his gaze from a tomb
and swung on the edge of silence
bearing the tortuous flare of skin.
I am told, not this, not touch,
he said, you may have me
but like light, under your heart.

MARILYN ON THE MOUNTAIN

Imagine a pucker in the raw clay
of the mountain's lower slopes, as though
a woman lay just beneath the surface
and turning in her sleep, gives vent
to all her decades' longing,
the muddied turbulence of her desire.

You fall on your knees near to where her
mouth is, water-hole in rusting terra-cotta
the lips a fringe of tiny ribs, a bird's
last testament; as though the sand has
worried all its force against dead flesh
leaving a dove's bones finely represented
drawn as an artist might, pronouncing
his arrival at the gates of intervention.

The mouth sings its bullet straight at the eye.
Within that charcoaled cup there lurks
her tongue, caged like the lion she once was
and the dried ridges of her crusted pout
spread a parched and threadbare fan
upon the earth, that flickered once in halls
and drawing-rooms, coding her heart's intent.

So do the clues gather; a breathless fossil-wing
faint as poppies, an upper lip familiar
as grass, the lower falling like a suicide
painted by the sun's late copper glaze.
The orifice shapes an invitation dark as opium.
I kneel like a devotee, trysting with dust.
A lizard-man, branding my life to meet her,
perfect trick of wind, an artifice of weather.

I drool at the icon underneath, her lust.
A silk saliva-skin moistens the edges of
that hollow into luminescence; I lick her
out of tombs, roll back the film for evidence.
A hot pink duplication peppers the air,
whirrs like a newsreel in my eyes creating doves.
The kiss burns its flint, runs a lava-current
into the bag of bones suspended over her.

Far off, I taste the heat of canyons, gorges,
sweet cactus-flowers; until a coat of sand
scrapes at my throat's cave, and memory
scrambles like a crazy beggar among the stones
offering its kiss to every feature in the conspiracy
of pipe-dreams, parchment and the land's loose mould.

ANGEL GRIEF

I have been wrestling with one word
all my life, one word, my life long.
It is not easy. It has the consistency
of bone in my waking hours, and just
when the wrist and the back of the hand
have its measure, why then it transforms
into the face of the one I loved
and so there is more to it than that
always more, the invitation stretching
from corridors and luminous white spaces
between leaves, between the print
and my own misfits, and finally also
between he and I, poised to make love
savage or slow burn, as we twist our
spirits over the table laden with words
trying to make a rope that will not fray
so much there is nothing left but the single
form of the word that is death, is the empty air.

THE LONG LIFE OF MISS CRAIG

If it was fire, the punishment, it took
my voice and gave it to the wood
and the wood took the shape of a ruler
in the four-square snapping hand
of the mistress of maths. She made
the equation fit, it burned my hand
exactly; two hands, a measured stick
of wood. And then the echo in a
chain of sound that was skin crying.

We've travelled this bruised century she
and I, Miss Craig of the pendulous breasts
the rod of wood her surrogate, love-lust
for my unpunishable palm. Stay calm
said my voice, scampering from the heat
and hiding in my shoes which kick Miss Craig
to bits; or finding refuge in the fist
which speaks instead, my head stupid under
rulers, file-dividers, multiplying breasts.

The cavernous bulk of Miss Craig and her tables
defies all measurement, though told in all
dimensions, seven times over, all-of-a-piece.
She lives in that cut in wood, the names
we carved her in, one capture for each day
she hammered down to size; we counted instead
her yellow teeth, the knuckles on her claw.
Fistfuls of songs like wedding-snow about
our hearts, we shove the knife in deep.

This table's circular, its angles missing,
voices rising now across an open vault
with music's looser weave for company.
A snail's message as I creep from under
desks, scrub off her ink and her geometry
to re-create my story in this poem's silver trail.

WILD CARD

There's a layer of frost on your
voice, was it something I said?
Is my petticoat showing
the one I danced in barefoot at
your wedding? Are you reminded
of anything? Well, I could
blow with my dragon's breath
you'd be all thawed out again
lit like the five fine stars
I wear on my black inky dress.

And while we're at it, did
you notice on the card I sent
at Christmas, how she'd stitched
initials to the silk and how
my threads trail over your base
gold, and I a silver ghost masking
and prompting, stretched over you;
how we gleam through one another
each time light catches us in
miniature, that one small corner
of a frame, the shelf it lands on
dusky somewhere in your house
I am sewn into; how Christmas
carries you among the images with
all its breath and bustle, an accident
of course, trick of a needle's craft.

Was it something I said, the
way I said it? Our rich patchwork
slapped into monotone stinging
my face. Perhaps I've lingered
too long in your shallows, crablike
beside a teeming underworld, scanning
it for clues, initials, signatures,
so strike out for the green bitch
ocean, a hair's breadth between
my hand waving in air like
the searching weed below, and yours.
I'd break in such tides, you said
but I missed the point; if I were you
you said, holding fast to the deck.

PROOFS

I suppose you could say it was like grit in my shoe
last week, as I walked slow-booted to the Court.
Money rattles to divert us and all the Magistrates are
solemn in their task. As though to feed his blame and my
pursuit, they fold their briefs in permanent adjournment.
I hadn't time to undo laces, flick the cinder-chip
back where it belonged. So it lodges in my heart
to work its will there; Jane's unborn wriggles to be out,
the central-heating clicks to automatic, my sleep is dust.
And all that loose-limbed coil of lust snakes a new route
across the morning roofs; Malcolm's back to Japanese
and won't be there to weave with me a wily garment
cunning enough to grow in, its hemp a fibrous network,
the pockets full of loose change and Malcolm's smile
a perfect etching on my man-sized linen handkerchief.

The world roams wide in company with shoes and aggravation;
night's cars interrupt my darkest oil and filter;
the wind gets up and blows my brothers to the four ends.
Sitting in Ewart Street and newly-mounted, the farthest one
(the first progenitor) stalks my hallway on his stick-legs.
At seventy and more he sends me letters from down under.
I scrutinise their drift from all that weight of air-miles
don't mind so much now being called a trooper,
chip-off-the-old-block, the one who made it home
though shedding husbands, notaries and vice along
the way; this story's nothing but an old-wives-tale
lopsided histories worrying my heels, still smarting
though it's twenty years or more since we first bent
                              the time to our delight.

GOOSE FLESH

We walked like two perfect strangers
in meadows made for love; the hot sting
of nettle, lush banks, seductive channels
dragging through the reeds. I trail my hand
in water, you don't touch. Or lean upon
your word, our eyes drift past each other.
Perhaps you see another ghosted over me
and I'm in love with all the sport of it
a canopy of heat, the lore of memory
as though to recreate my husband's eager
search among cow-parsley, roots and grasses
for our river-bed; we fled through years of
matrimony into the raw. Look, you say now
pointing to the pristine surface; a line
of geese glides downstream, perfect convoy
electric blue and green, stealing any
current we may have. Always it seems
you send our buried sex to do as it will
among the dragonflies. I hunt it there,
wait with my scarlet, scented flesh
for the next time, wishing we had a subtle
language of intent, discrete fold of a cuff,
flick of a fan, gesture precise as a bird's
tail to hint at temperature, then I'd not
burn so bright in the soft curve of rivers
going nowhere, transport for geese and fathomless.

DUBLIN IN AUGUST

I am sleeping over the top of commerce
my head beyond purchase
stretched to a line in a book that won't come straight
and when I move in a way that suggests
the direct approach
miss the mark altogether, can't find the house
with the name of a man I knew on the doorbell
a man who wrote and put it down straight
just as it was. No, I am not at all
matched to the commercial length
fall short of proper measurement.
My feet kick money all night long
from my father's pockets, instead
of love, and the shutters come down
on Talbot Street at night and suddenly
there is no-one there, no exchange
the stock has vanished behind metal ribs
and the ridged metallic shield of a final refusal
that makes of the night a steel forest to find you through
as I walk from John F. Keating's pub again
hunting again, searching among the sawdust
and the wild notes for a lost grieving voice
that will make the connection
when language seeped through the pores of the skin
and would not be stopped, even though
as she sings of it against the odds
the German students wave their steins
never once pausing in their never-ending march
of argument, and other nationalities
wrapped in nicotine and ersatz
fail to print her on their hearts
only sport the celtic t-shirt, read directions
follow the trail to each street lined with
music at the edge, to take the membrane home
a peeled-off transfer stuck upon a glass
see, here I was, my badge of authenticity

I took it in, six pubs, a wave of *nostalgie*
que j'aime. And I, attending with no suitable
regret, no worthwhile soft companion for my vigil
wait for shutters to close the city down
and the slow growth of lichen under the clothes
sweet shift of regained rot and spore
shooting voracious fingers into the frozen replica
of culture; boy, they buy it by the *punt.*

BETWEEN US

She wrote how difficult it was.
No news came, she had made a head
roughly, to stand in for him.
Tried to avoid the conventional thing,
wish you were here, having a lovely
but the words crumpled within themselves
like a paper bag and the fist inside.
Come back, she calls to her fleet
back into dark before I made you.
And they weighed, her words, heavy as
anchors, sinking slow to the sea-bed
just as the woman had given his head
only a borrowed light, a few vessels
of it, here and there. He belonged
she said, to the good warm dark,
she'd painted a black out of which
he came only fleeting, as though
bathed in lightning. She named him
The Glowing Man, as the world knows
only too well, illumination tires the eye
to blindness, it must come and go.
He is only just here, I can laugh
in such presence, it lays no
clamps upon me, it is the sweet
ephemeral taste you leave me; I know
as much of you in the after-glow
your face deepening in its absence
the great dark chime of a bell
ringing on after itself, my card
on a shelf you touch in passing
my head grown weary with the
stuck-fast print that cuts to the
bone. Wish you were here; she

carries forests, the lines of hills
in the bent form of herself, leaning
out; to hold land, contour, another she.
And her twin, opaque, rests in the shade
without him, without you. We are the
conjurors born out of lose. We fill you in.

(Inspired by the paintings of Naomi Frears, Tate Gallery St Ives)

LET'S PRETEND

I could have danced all night, except that
his fat thumb wore a pit in my clay shoulder
and the wax dripped from his nose and ran
like a skittering mercury ball down my laminated
bodice they called a boob-tube way back
when plastic was the exception not the rule.
I trod on his lumpen shoes with my wicked
little swords they call stilettos, but he
didn't wince, took it like a lamb, sacrificially.

There wasn't much room on the dance-floor.
You could smell marshmallow and the kippery
tang of sex. I'd guess a dozen digits poked
their triumphant march into dry ditches
though mine dribbled a bit when he tickled my
rhinestone drop, missing the lobe by an inch.
I'm used to it, the game of catch, imagination
rubbed into flame, though his blind tongue
curled a cool blue cavern in my reluctant ear.

I spat on the floor and it flashed like malachite.
His dreams adrift, my prince's glistening head is
bolted to my breast, our bed of moss, his ass's milk
grunting his nightly raid on the world's dumb-show.
Rivers ooze between us, broken flood down his
trousers' seam and my scarlet stitches, rare as
a goat's song, angel grief, the play as long as ghosts
of us can dance together differently, pretend
it isn't so. What do they call epiphany these days,

could be a strobe's trick, flying ribbons of
our flesh; or not even that small measure, only
the rag and bone features of a city, cobbled together
like one of those models my dad used to love,
wings of a plane so fine they might break in
two if you tried to fly it, glue hardened
into opaque ribs of amber; and how he wouldn't
stop, his eyes ahead of it over the lake.
I feel his fingers lock upon the spine
send my desire back down the century to land
at his feet, their shoes tight, all I can see.

JUST BEFORE

See, there is still time, it is not come
early cracking the roof, or a splinter
of wind through the boards. A mouse
tracks time somewhere I cannot reach,
the room is a crepuscule, I have
pulled its skein towards me as though
winding wool for a grandmother,
the kind whose time does not crack
every minute or so, and the hank
sits on her blue and purple wrists
and the twitch of her arm is regular
as a metronome. I knew music through
and through her, the song was not
stoppered as though for blasphemy.
See, I have flung my skein around
your heart, can you feel the tug, tug
as I stand on my rock, still in time
though the vast stars shape eternities
for us, and who's to know where it might
go, this way and that, cat's-cradle.

ATTIC

Locked in a room, in a house, somewhere
between King's Cross and the Northern Line
all you own of city is a cube of air.
Some days its blank white stare is
sky from the attic's point of view,
relentless vacancy after closing-time,
the city's cool white heart teeming
with microscopic cultures, virus and
atom, ant and molecule, a wing flips
once against your eye and there is lilac
field and bird, world in four dimensions
breaking its symmetry for a fifth,
the city's simulation, neon, hieroglyph,
imaginations birth, and executioner.

SLOW FUSE

Tate Gallery St Ives

At the beginning, where a stone curves on itself
and marks the base, your heel reminds me
of a snail. We are starting to climb the steps
as words slip their moorings and float aloft,
Porthmeor a great stroke of sun upon
the back of us. At the beginning, a daughter
curled like this monument, all her colours
coming to birth two decades on, the Heron window
spreading her lights, the snail of poetry forever
coiling at our hearts. See how it climbs these
new white steps, stone-washed, a slow thing
taking its time; your tread upon the back of me
a slow thing, footprints worn deep into my shell
and the voice now thin as a gull and cracked
on so much tide, and never a dull moment here
until now. To cut a story short, we start
to climb the bleached steps, the only history
swarming in my eye that matches this to yours –
a snail-shape echoed in the vaults of you.

If I was married here, it took a long time.
The horns twitch, the syllables part company
along the way. A white lace dress floats
across the bay, as though our nuptials took place
behind a curtain. You in London, me in St Ives,
our messages uncertain. Such light deserves a kiss.
I plant one on the card, lick the stamp and buckle
on my boots. The white stone isn't kind to snails,
the spiralling within my skull is ravishing.
If we're to tilt and crawl, if we must slither up,
we'll need to bolt our meanings back into their
clasps. I'm not sure, love, although the gallery

houses all my early company – the wild explorers
who dared this land ahead of me; being a little
slow you see, arrived so late in love, so life-encrusted,
my Alfred Wallis card is bone-dry, rattles in the box.

THE PATH FROM YOU BACK TO ME

You said, you must squeeze the olive
gently, and with that growl you have
that coats the words in goats' hide.
You are sitting close, I can feel
hairs rise on your arms like stalks
in a wind; it was not the lark
took me home, that dawning bird
though it sang like the queen you
said I was, walking straight; wine
busied itself with my blood, forcing
an accident of birth. I was torn in
my leaving, as though you had pressed
warm oil from your olive-skin into
my heart. All I had done was to ask
of her, the room running in reverse
her smile the firm rich pout of a
conqueror, I am lame at her foot.
You burn, it is a leaf falling, not a
glove. I try for the decent thing
four o'clock exit, ever with nightingales
their midnight cloak worn loose
across these hours; we are flame to
the new year, a pestilence cowering in
the grate. Our hostess kicks a coal,
my question is a bellows, thin air
is all I catch, press her silence into
thick silken ropes and choke on it.
Olives, you said, you must squeeze
them like this, for their yield.
Even so I own the wide world entire,
stealing a few for my passage across
the field, the only one at dawn
to know how best to leave a brother
before we fall like gloves, or rotten fruit.

Other books in the same series include

KEVIN CROSSLEY-HOLLAND   *Poems from East Anglia*

MARTYN CRUCEFIX   *A Madder Ghost*

HILARY DAVIES   *In a Valley of This Restless Mind*

DAVID GASCOYNE   *Encounter with Silence*

DAVID GASCOYNE   *Selected Prose 1934-1996*

GARY GEDDES   *Flying Blind*

PHOEBE HESKETH   *A Box of Silver Birch*

JEREMY HOOKER   *Our Lady of Europe*

JUDITH KAZANTZIS   *Swimming Through the Grand Hotel*

BLAKE MORRISON & PAULA REGO   *Pendle Witches*

VICTOR PASMORE   *The Man Within*

PASCALE PETIT   *Heart of a Deer*

MYRA SCHNEIDER   *The Panic Bird*

ANTHONY THWAITE   *Selected Poems 1956-1996*

EDWARD UPWARD   *Remembering the Earlier Auden*

EDWARD UPWARD   *The Scenic Railway*

Please write to Enitharmon Press for a full catalogue